SCHOOL GIRLS; OR, THE AFRICAN MEAN GIRLS PLAY

BY JOCELYN BIOH

★

★

DRAMATISTS
PLAY SERVICE
INC.

To JC—thank you for fighting for me and this play.
It worked.
Love you girl.

SCHOOL GIRLS; OR, THE AFRICAN MEAN GIRLS PLAY had its world premiere at MCC Theater (Robert LuPone, Bernard Telsey, and William Cantler, Artistic Directors; Blake West, Executive Director) on October 16, 2017. It was directed by Rebecca Taichman, the set design was by Arnulfo Maldonado, the costume design was by Dede M. Ayite, the lighting design was by Jen Schriever, the sound design was by Palmer Hefferan, the dialect coach was Deborah Hecht, and the production stage manager was Laura Wilson. The cast was as follows:

PAULINA SARPONG	MaameYaa Boafo
ERICKA BOAFO	Nabiyah Be
AMA	Níke Kadri
NANA	Abena Mensah-Bonsu
MERCY	Mirirai Sithole
GIFTY	Paige Gilbert
HEADMISTRESS FRANCIS	Myra Lucretia Taylor
ELOISE AMPONSAH	Zainab Jah

PLAYWRIGHT'S NOTE

In 2011, the Miss Ghana pageant officials, in an attempt to become the first West African country to have a viable and perhaps winning contestant in the Miss Universe pageant, named Yayra Erica Nego (an American-born and Minnesota-raised biracial woman) the winner of the Miss Ghana pageant. Officials claimed that her father was from the Volta Region of Ghana (a region that is considered extremely obscure, and rarely have people ever emigrated from there) but never confirmed his name or whereabouts before procuring her as a contestant for the Miss Ghana pageant. She beat out two of Ghana's most famous models at the time. Erica went on to the Miss Universe pageant that year where she did not place. I thought that story was pretty damn interesting... So I wrote a play inspired by it.

CHARACTERS

(All characters are of West African descent and are to be played by African and/or Black actors. Thank you.)

PAULINA SARPONG *(Paul-LEE-nah SAAR-pong)*. 18 years old; the most popular girl in school and knows it. She is beautiful, talented, vindictive, yet somehow loveable.

ERICKA BOAFO *(BWAH-foh)*. 18 years old; Light/fair skin. She is a transfer student and is new to school. She is enchanting, sweet, elusive. *(NOTE: Should be played by a fair-skinned biracial [Black and White] woman.)*

AMA *(Ahh-mah)*. 18 years old; the sensible, smart one of Paulina's pack and has the honor of being her best friend. Her loyalty to Paulina is starting to fray, and she has to work up towards being the girl who is not afraid to say it like she means it.

NANA *(Nah-nah)*. 16 years old; the quiet, simple, and sensitive one of Paulina's pack. She never means any harm and strives to do the right thing. She struggles with her love of food and snacks.

MERCY. 16 years old; the witty sidekick to Gifty and will do and say anything to stay a member of Paulina's pack.

GIFTY. 16 years old; the "Frick" to Mercy's "Frack"; loves being part of Paulina's pack and will do anything to be considered cool.

HEADMISTRESS FRANCIS. 40s; the Headmistress of Aburi Girls Boarding School; loves her students and will do whatever she can to both uplift and protect them.

ELOISE AMPONSAH *(Ell-oh-eez Amm-pohn-saah)*. 40s; Extremely poised and well-mannered former Miss Ghana 1966. She is now a recruiter for the Miss Ghana pageant. She speaks with a slightly affected British accent and prides herself in always being a lady.

SETTING and TIME

Aburi *(EHH-bree)* Girls' boarding school—located in the Aburi mountains in central Ghana. The year is 1986.

SCHOOL GIRLS;
OR, THE AFRICAN MEAN GIRLS PLAY

PART ONE

Breakfast at Aburi Girls School. The "crew": Paulina, Ama, Nana, Mercy, and Gifty sit at a lunch table. They are Thee Popular Crew and everyone knows it.

PAULINA. Seriously Nana? After all I've said, you are still eating porridge?

MERCY. Yeah, is this your idea of a diet?

NANA. Well, it's a smaller portion.

PAULINA. Are you determined to look like a cow?

ALL GIRLS. *(Except Nana.)* Ha!/A cow!/Farm animals!

    The girls all giggle.

PAULINA. Listen Nana, I don't know how many times I have to say it:

    She snaps at Mercy to cue her.

MERCY. "We have a reputation to maintain."

GIFTY. "To stay fit."

MERCY. "Looking fine-fine."

GIFTY. "All the time."

PAULINA. Listen, I get it—you never got to eat what you wanted when you were younger—

MERCY. But you can't make up for lost time now.

GIFTY. Yeah, the time is lost.

PAULINA. So…do you want to be fat-fat? Or fit and popular?

MERCY and GIFTY. Yeah, choose your choice.

NANA. Umm…popular.

PAULINA. Good… Then let me help you make smarter choices. I need an apple anyway.

MERCY. Oh, we can get it for you Paulina.

PAULINA. No, no, it's fine. I'm trying to burn some more calories.

Paulina leaves.

MERCY. Sorry Nana.

GIFTY. Yeah, sorry.

MERCY. We just don't want her coming after us.

NANA. No, I get it.

AMA. She has been acting so crazy lately.

MERCY. I know—this pageant! She's always judging everything.

GIFTY. *(Imitating Paulina.)* "You like your hair like that?"

MERCY. "Those shoes are hideous."

GIFTY. "You know girls… Apples are a very good source of fiber!"

MERCY. Like we know what fiber is!

NANA. She's just looking out for us. Like she always has.

AMA. Looking out for us? Please!

MERCY and GIFTY. Oooh, yeah.

MERCY. I still can't believe you were able to forgive her, Ama.

GIFTY. Forgiveness.

MERCY. Had that got back to your father—

GIFTY. A pastor—

MERCY. Who knows what would have happened.

GIFTY. Crucifixion!

AMA. Can we not bring that up right now?

MERCY. Fine.   GIFTY. Sorry.

AMA. She's just acting up because her and Kofi broke up again.

NANA. No, she told me they're back together now.

AMA. Whatever. I can't keep up anymore.

MERCY. Well, she promised me and Gifty dresses for the audition. So I won't ruffle too many feathers before then.

GIFTY. "Feathers."

AMA. *(To Mercy/Gifty.)* But your father can afford to get you and Gifty any dress you want already.

MERCY. But you know he won't get us frivolous things!

GIFTY. And to him, dresses from America?: Frivolous!

MERCY. We know we won't be picked, but we can at least look good.

AMA. Whatever. Paulina only made us all sign up to audition because Headmistress said there needed to be at least five names on the list.

NANA. But we could have a chance.

AMA. Please Nana, no one ever stands a chance when it comes to Paulina.

> *Paulina reenters.*

PAULINA. And don't you forget it!

ALL GIRLS. Paulina! / Welcome back! / We missed you.

PAULINA. *(Hands Nana an apple.)* Here you are Nana.

NANA. Oh, thanks Paulina.

PAULINA. I got you the smallest one. I can't say it enough ladies: Regulation is your friend.

AMA. Totally.

MERCY. Our friend.

GIFTY. Our best friend. Other than you of course, Paulina.

PAULINA. Awww, you are so sweet Gifty.

GIFTY. Thank you Paulina.

PAULINA. *(Takes bite of her apple.)* You know girls, apples are a very good source of fiber. My American cousins told me there is a parable there that says: "An apple a week keeps you from being sick."

NANA. *(Takes a bite.)* Yeah… They're really good.

GIFTY. *(To Nana.)* They keep you from being sick.

PAULINA. Portion control Nana…

> *Nana stops eating and puts the apple down.*

(Moving on.) Ugh… I'm so tired this morning. Can you see it under my eyes? *(Pulls down her "eye bags.")* Tired, right?

MERCY, GIFTY, and AMA. What?! No!/Are you kidding?!/You? Never!

PAULINA. Really? Well, I was up all night writing a letter to my Kofi.

     The girls all swoon.

MERCY. Oh, how is he? Is his training going well? I'm glad you're back together.

GIFTY. Don't you miss him?

PAULINA. Of course I miss him. But if I'm going to be married

MERCY, GIFTY, and AMA. Oooh / Awww / Eh-eh, married where?

PAULINA. Well, eventually be married to a potential soccer player, then I have to get used to us being away from each other.

MERCY. But he's planning to come to the big dance, yes?

PAULINA. Of course! He can't wait. I am really looking forward to you all meeting him.

AMA. Oh, so he is definitely going to come this time? He's missed the last two.

PAULINA. Because he was busy—like I said.

AMA. Right.

MERCY. And what about you Ama? Is your Osei* going to come?

AMA. *(Blushing.)* Yes, he is.

     The girls all giggle (except Paulina).

MERCY. I'm telling you Ama, Osei is so fine.

GIFTY. So fine!

MERCY. That skin, that smile, that body?!

GIFTY. Perfect.

MERCY. You are a lucky one, eh.

AMA. Thanks girls.

PAULINA. Yes, well let's just hope he keeps his eyes fixed on you this time.

AMA. Pardon?

---

* Pronounced "OHH-say."

10

PAULINA. Oh, I didn't want to make a big deal about it, but he was practically all over me at the last dance.

AMA. I didn't see any of that.

PAULINA. Well you wouldn't. He must be one of those slick ones—a womanizer.

GIFTY. *(Confused about what to say.)* Yeah… A womanizer.

MERCY. *(Let's change the subject.)* So, Paulina. Have you decided what you are going to wear for the Miss Ghana audition?

GIFTY. Are you making a dress for yourself again? Your designs are so gorgeous.

MERCY. Or are you wearing something you cousins in America gave you? I can't believe how many options they sent.

AMA. Yeah, it was a lot.

PAULINA. I know. Well you know my Auntie Salo works at that high class restaurant I was telling you about.

MERCY. Ah yes, White Castle.

GIFTY. A castle with food.

PAULINA. And she is always shopping for me at all the trendy American boutiques. Conway. Walmart. The list goes on. But since this is such a big moment in my life, she sent me an outfit purchased at the most famous retail place in all of New York City.

MERCY. *(Amazed.)* Where?   GIFTY. Where is that?

PAULINA. Chinatown!

MERCY, NANA, and GIFTY. Wow/Oh my goodness/There is a China in New York?!

PAULINA. That's right ladies. I will be wearing my very own Calvin Klean dress to the dance.

MERCY. Oh my goodness!

GIFTY. I don't even know who that is!

NANA. I am so jealous of your life Paulina.

PAULINA. I know. I'm so blessed.

AMA. Yeah, you really are.

PAULINA. Oh Ama, don't worry. I know you can't afford to get a nice dress for yourself, so I'll let you wear one of my options. I'm sure one of them will fit you.

AMA. Uh, thanks Paulina, but I think I'll be okay.

PAULINA. Are you sure? I mean, you're my best friend and I really need you to look good Ama.

An awkward beat.

MERCY. *(Trying to cool things down again.)* You are so thoughtful Paulina! Giving us ALL dresses.

GIFTY. What are we going to do without you when you and Ama graduate?

PAULINA. I don't know. So take this last year to soak up my wisdom.

AMA. Or maybe you girls will be just fine on your own? Thinking for yourselves is not hard you know?

MERCY. Eh-eh. Think for myself?

GIFTY. Why would I do that?

PAULINA. And what is that supposed to mean Ama?

AMA. I'm just saying that they are smart girls and they don't need to follow anyone—

PAULINA. —I just think they appreciate that I protect them! Like how people make fun of Mercy because her rich daddy won't buy her new shoes.

MERCY. He's very…frugal.

PAULINA. Or the way people talk about Gifty now that she's had to repeat her first year.

GIFTY. Not cool.

PAULINA. And Nana here: who ate lunch every day by herself until I brought her into the group. Finally giving her some friends. Isn't that right Nana?

NANA. Yes.

AMA. Look Paulina, I'm not trying to start anything, okay?

PAULINA. Are you sure? Look, you're not still mad about that thing are you? I thought we were over it.

AMA. I am… We are.

PAULINA. Good.

> *Headmistress Francis walks into the cafeteria. Paulina turns on her "public face" charm.*

HEADMISTRESS FRANCIS. Oh, good morning girls.

ALL GIRLS. Good morning Headmistress.

PAULINA. How are you this morning Headmistress?

HEADMISTRESS FRANCIS. I'm well, thank you. A bit busy this morning. We have a new student coming in today.

> *That's a surprise to everyone.*

AMA. Really? We're already in our second week of school.

HEADMISTRESS FRANCIS. I know. So I trust you all will help in getting her settled quickly, yes?

ALL GIRLS. Yes/Of course Headmistress./For sure.

PAULINA. What a week we're having! We were just talking about how excited we all are about the Miss Ghana recruiter coming tomorrow. Isn't that right, ladies?

ALL GIRLS. Yes!/We can't wait!/I'm so nervous.

MERCY. How many girls will they be selecting?

GIFTY. Is it true that it's only one?

HEADMISTRESS FRANCIS. Yes, only one.

GIFTY. *(To Mercy.)* I told you!

PAULINA. And if she wins that, then she'll go on to the Miss Global Universe pageant with girls from all over the world!

ALL GIRLS. Ahhh!/That is so amazing!/All over the world?!/Wow!

HEADMISTRESS FRANCIS. Now, I am not a big fan of competitions myself, you know what I always say:

ALL GIRLS. "Education is the only gift that no one can take away."

HEADMISTRESS FRANCIS. That's right. And I want you all to remember, that even if you are not selected, it is not the end of the world. God still loves you! Amen?

ALL GIRLS. Amen.

HEADMISTRESS FRANCIS. Good.

MERCY. But Paulina, you ARE going to be Miss Ghana 1986!

NANA. Yes, of course! We all know that you are most beautiful girl here at Aburi.

AMA. Yeah…

PAULINA. *(Coy.)* Well…

HEADMISTRESS FRANCIS. Okay…now girls—

MERCY. —And no one from West Africa has ever made it to the top of the Miss Global Universe pageant.

HEADMISTRESS FRANCIS. Is that so?

GIFTY. Yes! It is always some girl from South Africa or Ethiopia.

NANA. Eh-eh! You remember when the winner from Namibia was a white?!

HEADMISTRESS FRANCIS. A white?

AMA. Well, they said that she was born and raised there, so technically, she is African.

MERCY. Oh, so then it would be no problem if the winner of Miss Italy had black skin?

GIFTY. Oh please! You know there would be many problems with that—

NANA. —She probably wouldn't even make it to the stage—

MERCY. —That is what I am saying—

AMA. —I'm just letting you know how they got around the rules!

HEADMISTRESS FRANCIS. —Okay, calm down girls—

NANA. —But you know what else I heard?!

ALL GIRLS. What?!

NANA. That this year's winner will accompany Bobby Brown to an American awards show!

MERCY, GIFTY, AMA, and NANA. BOBBY BROWN!!!!/Ahhh!/I would die!

HEADMISTRESS FRANCIS. Eh, girls! Inside voices please!

MERCY. Oh my God if I could listen to "Mr. Telephone Man" a million times a day, I would!

GIFTY. Me too!

HEADMISTRESS FRANCIS. Me three! That song is my JAM!

ALL GIRLS. *(Excitement that she knows the song.)* AYYYYE!/
HEADMISTRESS!/LOOK AT YOU, OH!

> *Headmistress exits. The girls settle down.*

NANA. Wow Paulina. You will be in all the American magazines!
Eating at fancy restaurants.

MERCY. Rubbing elbows with famous people.

GIFTY. Elbows!

PAULINA. I know.

AMA. Don't you think Kofi would mind?

PAULINA. Of course not. He would not want to interfere with my
modeling career.

AMA. You say what?

PAULINA. Modeling. That's the plan after I graduate you know.
Become the next Iman. College is cute, but I'm thinking about my
future realistically.

MERCY. Listen, I'm sure that Kofi is going to be very excited to tell
everyone that he is with the most beautiful woman in Ghana…

GIFTY. Ghana!

MERCY. Or in the whole world.

GIFTY. Universe!

PAULINA. *(Feigned humility.)* Ladies… Please.

GIFTY. It is true! Who else could beat you?

> *Headmistress reenters the cafeteria with a new girl, Ericka.
> Everyone stares in shock.*

HEADMISTRESS FRANCIS. Girls, I would like you all to meet
Ericka Boafo. She has just transferred into Aburi.

ERICKA. Hello everyone.

ALL GIRLS. Hi.

HEADMISTRESS FRANCIS. Ericka, this is Gifty, Paulina, Mercy,
Ama, and Nana. Paulina and Ama here are in their last year as well.

PAULINA. Welcome to Aburi Ericka.

ERICKA. Thank you.

HEADMISTRESS FRANCIS. Ericka is joining us all the way from

The States!

MERCY. The United States of America?

GIFTY. So are you a white?

HEADMISTRESS FRANCIS. Gifty!

ERICKA. No, it's fine Headmistress. I am a little pale. Clearly, I have been missing some of that good African sun.

All the girls, except Paulina, laugh. They like her already.

HEADMISTRESS FRANCIS. I'm sorry for the quick tour. I need to go and set up some classrooms—we're a bit short-staffed today. But if you need anything Ericka, please don't hesitate to ask.

ERICKA. Thank you Headmistress but I'm sure I'll be fine.

PAULINA. Yes, we'll take good care of her.

HEADMISTRESS FRANCIS. Lovely. See you all soon.

Headmistress exits.

PAULINA. Please, Ericka. Have a seat.

ERICKA. Thank you.

The girls all move down to make room for Ericka. A small beat of awkward silence as they all stare at her.

PAULINA. So… You're from America?

ERICKA. Yes. Well, no. I mean…I'm Ghanaian. I've just been living in the States for a while.

PAULINA. Oh, well that's exciting. I have some cousins who live there as well.

ERICKA. Really? Where?

PAULINA. *(She doesn't know where.)* Like…all over.

AMA. Where did you live?

ERICKA. I went to school in the Midwest area. Ohio.

MERCY. Ohio.

GIFTY. I've never even heard of that one before.

ERICKA. It's nothing special.

NANA. Aren't your cousins from New York, Paulina?

GIFTY. Is that near Ohio?

16

PAULINA. Yeah. They're in New York. And all over America. Like I said.

AMA. And you're in your last year as well?

ERICKA. I am. I hope I haven't missed too much. I know you all started classes a week ago.

AMA. I'm sure you'll catch up.

ERICKA. I appreciate Headmistress making an exception for me.

PAULINA. A special exception it seems. What do your parents do?

ERICKA. Oh, my dad has a company… A cocoa factory actually.

AMA. Boafo? As in Boafo Cocoa Farms?

ERICKA. Yes, you know it?

The girls all know that company. They are impressed.

MERCY. *(Sotto voce.)* Oh, they make some GOOD cocoa!

GIFTY. *(Sotto voce.)* Chocolate.

AMA. Yes, of course. My boyfriend works at that dairy farm.

ERICKA. He does? Oh you must be talking about, ummm…

AMA. Osei.

ERICKA. Right.

AMA. You know him?

ERICKA. Not really, but I think I've seen him around.

AMA. Osei says that your parents travel a lot—he rarely even sees them.

ERICKA. Yeah, he's right—they are always busy traveling. The schedule was becoming too much. Transferring schools all the time. So we decided that I should finish my schooling here in his hometown.

PAULINA. So when was the last time you were here?

ERICKA. I can't even tell you. So, forgive me. It's going to take me a while to get my accent and get used to the heat.

The girls all laugh. Except Paulina.

MERCY. I'm sorry Ericka, but I have to ask: What did you use to get your hair that long?

ERICKA. Oh, this is just natural.

GIFTY. Wow. You are so lucky.

ERICKA. Thanks but Headmistress scheduled my haircut for next week.

PAULINA. I mean, mine is that long too. When I straighten it, you can see—

NANA. —I wish my hair was easier to manage.

ERICKA. Well, I have tons of products you could try—a bunch of things that I got in America.

NANA. Ooh, like what? Hair grease?

MERCY. Oil?

AMA. Lotion?

ERICKA. All of that. You girls should come to my dormitory and try them out. We can have a little makeover party or something.

MERCY. Oooh, a makeover party.

GIFTY. A party to get made over!

NANA. Count me in!

AMA. Yeah, I want to try everything.

GIFTY. 'Cause your stuff must be top quality!

MERCY. Clearly! Even the Caro Light they have in The States must be top shelf. You don't even have any blemishes!

ERICKA. The what?

MERCY. You know? The cream.

GIFTY. Bleaching cream.

MERCY. The ones they sell here will just burn your skin off.

GIFTY. Fire.

MERCY. And they give really bad blisters.

GIFTY. Nasty.

ERICKA. Oh, well—

MERCY. —But I would love to try yours! It seems like it works really good.

GIFTY. Quality.

ERICKA. Oh, no. I don't use… I mean, this is just my natural tone.

18

GIFTY. Wow. You really are blessed.

MERCY. Our other cousin has lighter skin too.

GIFTY. She's albino!

MERCY. It's still light!

GIFTY. Anyway, I can't wait for this party! Are you free after class today? Oooh! Do you have a boombox? The one I had broke down.

AMA. That thing never worked Gifty.

GIFTY. It did! *(Under breath.)* You just had to hold the plug in place and it was fine…

MERCY. *(Under breath.)* Let it go Gifty.

ERICKA. I do have one actually! And I brought some new music with me too.

MERCY. Do you know of Bobby Brown?

ERICKA. Are you kidding? I love him! I went to a New Edition concert last year.

ALL GIRLS. YOU DID?!

ERICKA. Yeah, I even have a poster that he signed.

MERCY. Oh my goodness!

GIFTY. He signed a poster!

NANA. And she has it!

ALL GIRLS. AHHH!

PAULINA. You have to forgive them Ericka. We don't always get such fancy new students like you in our school—with your music and lotions and makeup.

MERCY. All the things we need to look good for the recruiter!

ERICKA. Recruiter?

GIFTY. For the Miss Ghana pageant!

ERICKA. Oh yeah! I saw that list in the front office. I signed up for it. Looks like fun!

> *Small beat. Uh-oh.*

MERCY. *(Trying to cut through the tension.)* It is going to be fun!

NANA. *(Without even thinking.)* And you can definitely be the next Miss Ghana.

PAULINA. *(To Nana.)* Oh really?

NANA. I mean—

ERICKA. Yeah, I thought it might be a fun way to make some friends.

PAULINA. Oh, so you are not really that interested?

ERICKA. Well, I've never thought about beauty pageants before.

AMA. Surely someone has told you that you are perfect for modeling or something.

ERICKA. I mean maybe once or twice.

PAULINA. But now you are seriously thinking about it?

ERICKA. I guess so.

AMA. It's just a pageant. What do you have to lose?

PAULINA. *(Laughs.)* Well, other than to me. Obviously.

ERICKA. Right…

> Beat. Something's going on here.

PAULINA. So do you have a boyfriend Ericka?

ERICKA. Not anymore—

PAULINA. —'Cause I do! Kofi. He's in Kumasi training with the Ghana Black Stars. He's a soccer player. He's even been to the World Cup.

ERICKA. That's nice.

MERCY and GIFTY. *(Sotto voce.)* World Cup?

PAULINA. But you don't have a boyfriend, huh?

ERICKA. I've just been focused on my studies and my extracurriculars.

AMA. Well you should join the show choir. We're all in it. Well, it's just us. But it's really fun.

ERICKA. Oh yeah?

MERCY. And sometimes Headmistress lets us pick our songs.

GIFTY. Like the one we're working on now.

MERCY. We've been rehearsing all week!

GIFTY. And she is letting us perform it for the recruiter as part of the auditions.

MERCY. Since we all have solos!

GIFTY. Which is special—since Paulina usually gets those.

PAULINA. Actually, I'm the LEAD soloist. For the past two years.

ERICKA. Oh that's nice. You must be really good.

PAULINA. I am. Headmistress likes to make everyone feel like they have a fair chance, but we all know I'm the best. These girls sing like hyenas.

> *Paulina laughs. No one joins her—or if they do, it's half-hearted. The school bell chimes.*

ERICKA. I should probably get to class. I just wish I knew where I was going though.

MERCY. Oh, what room are you looking for?

ERICKA. 138—Advanced Algebra?

AMA. Oh, I have that class too. I'll show you the way.

ERICKA. Oh great, thanks. If nothing else, I'm glad I know how to get to the most important place on campus.

NANA. Where is that?

ERICKA. The cafeteria! I'm so greedy, I already can't wait for lunch.

> *The girls laugh. Ericka, Mercy, Gifty, and Ama all walk off to class. Paulina pulls Nana to the side before she can follow them.*

PAULINA. So Nana, have you forgotten where your loyalty lies?

NANA. What? You know I am always nice with everyone.

PAULINA. I don't give a shit about nice! There's no room for that in this group, you hear me?

> *Nana is silent.*

(*Snaps fingers.*) Hello? Do you hear me? Or do you have food stuffed in your ears too, you fucking cow!

NANA. Yes, I hear you.

PAULINA. Now, since you keep getting caught with snacks in class, you have another detention after school today, yes?

NANA. Yes.

PAULINA. Good. Because I need you to sneak into Headmistress's files and pull Ericka's out for me.

NANA. What?!

PAULINA. You heard me.

NANA. Paulina, I can't do that. Do you know how much trouble I could get in if Headmistress found out?

PAULINA. Do I look like I care?

NANA. What do you even need with her files anyway?

PAULINA. That's none of your business.

NANA. Well, you're going to have to ask someone else because I can't do that Paulina. Headmistress has already warned me that if I get any more detentions, it is going to affect me getting into college. And you know how much that means to me. I would be the first in my family.

PAULINA. Well it obviously doesn't mean enough.

> *Paulina reaches into Nana's top and pulls out a small bread roll.*

NANA. Paulina, no. Please. Give it back!

PAULINA. *(Mocking.)* "Oh Paulina please, just let me eat. I just want to go to college!" Give me a fucking break, okay?!

> *Paulina throws the bread on the floor.*

NANA. *(Looks down in shame.)* I'm just hungry.

PAULINA. Then eat… I'll just tell Headmistress about all the places you're stashing food. Then you'll get more detentions. And maybe expelled. And I know you don't want to be sent back to your mother with the way she likes to starve you. I mean, I can't blame her. I'd be ashamed if I had a fat-ass daughter too.

NANA. Paulina, please. I can't do that—

PAULINA. But you can avoid all of that strife, if you just get me Ericka's files. Like I told you to do the first damn time… Do we have an understanding now?

NANA. *(Eventually.)* Yes.

PAULINA. Good. Oh, and don't get caught!

> *Paulina walks off. After a moment, Nana picks up the bread and stuffs it back in her shirt.*

PART TWO

Headmistress Francis sits at a lunch table in the cafeteria. She is going over some papers. Eloise, elegantly dressed, enters.

ELOISE. *(Slightly affected British accent.)* Francis Adwoa* Frimpong! Look at you!

HEADMISTRESS FRANCIS. Eloise?

ELOISE. I asked some students where I could find you and they said the cafeteria—

HEADMISTRESS FRANCIS. —Yes, I'm just doing a bit of food inventory—

ELOISE. —Of course you are. Oh Franny. Come here! It's so good to see you!

An awkward hug.

HEADMISTRESS FRANCIS. Yes. Quite the surprise.

ELOISE. Whew, let me just catch my breath for second. I can't tell you the last time I have been up here in the Aburi mountains.

HEADMISTRESS FRANCIS. Ah yes, it is definitely a workout.

ELOISE. I can't believe we used to race up these hills every day! Feels like one hundred years ago, right?

HEADMISTRESS FRANCIS. Sometimes…

ELOISE. …Right.

HEADMISTRESS FRANCIS. Pardon me Eloise…but what are you doing here?

ELOISE. Darling, I'm one of the recruiters for the Miss Ghana pageant.

HEADMISTRESS FRANCIS. Oh, well isn't that a coincidence? We weren't expecting you until tomorrow.

ELOISE. Yes, I know. But Aburi was the last school on my list, so I decided to come up earlier, go see my mum and some family— make a trip of it, you know? I haven't been back home in over ten years. Can you believe that?

* "Ah-joo-ah"

HEADMISTRESS FRANCIS. Yes I can.

ELOISE. Anyway, I am so excited to be a recruiter this year. I feel very committed to finding a winning girl. You know—and I don't mean to brag—

HEADMISTRESS FRANCIS. You? Of course not—

ELOISE. —But if one of my recruits becomes Miss Ghana 1986, I will get a big promotion!

HEADMISTRESS FRANCIS. Really?

ELOISE. And you know what that means?

HEADMISTRESS FRANCIS. Uhh, a bigger crown?

ELOISE. No, it means big, big, big money! For both myself, the winner, AND a generous donation to the school—in this case, Aburi.

HEADMISTRESS FRANCIS. Oh, I was not aware of that.

ELOISE. I know that, love. It's my job to tell you.

HEADMISTRESS FRANCIS. That would be wonderful. Things have become a bit tight around here. I am managing, but you know, we could always use some help.

ELOISE. Yes, I heard about girls testing pretty low in recent years, budget cuts, missionaries pulling their funding.

HEADMISTRESS FRANCIS. We're managing. Trust me.

ELOISE. Of course you are. Getting a few girls to work off their detentions with manual labor, eh? Headmistress Mary used to pull those same stunts when we were students here.

HEADMISTRESS FRANCIS. Oh no, I'm just trying to teach the girls responsibility and—

ELOISE. Oh don't take offense Franny! It was a joke. But seriously, if we find the right girl here: She wins. I win. And Aburi Girls School gets a big old paycheck. Doesn't that sound great?

HEADMISTRESS FRANCIS. It does.

ELOISE. God only knows how much of your own personal money you have poured into this place.

HEADMISTRESS FRANCIS. I love this school Eloise. I don't mind the sacrifice.

ELOISE. Awww… *(Moving on.)* But, let's get to the matter at hand, eh? The girls.

HEADMISTRESS FRANCIS. Well, they are all very excited.

ELOISE. I remember when I was first discovered. Selling mangos at my mother's fruit stand when a recruiter just spotted me. It was a wondrous time in my life. That is, until the day I was crowned Miss Ghana of course.

HEADMISTRESS FRANCIS. And you represented our country with much pride.

ELOISE. And I hope to give some lucky young lady here the same chance… You know, it's funny because, as I was passing through, I happened to notice a lovely young lady.

HEADMISTRESS FRANCIS. Oh?

ELOISE. She is absolutely gorgeous. Ye' tall, brownish hair, lovely shape… *(Eventually.)* Fair skinned.

HEADMISTRESS FRANCIS. Ah, you must be talking about Ericka. She has just transferred into the school.

ELOISE. Well she is absolutely perfect for the pageant. As I said, I have turned over every rock and shook down every bush in Ghana it seems—honestly, I was getting desperate. But alas, God provides!

HEADMISTRESS FRANCIS. All the time.

ELOISE. Now she's a girl who can actually stand a chance against the likes of beauty queens from Spain, Brazil, France, or Colombia.

HEADMISTRESS FRANCIS. Well yes, she's lovely, but I think many of my girls would.

ELOISE. You know… It has become clear that MGU judges are fond of girls who have a more universal and commercial look.

HEADMISTRESS FRANCIS. So… You are saying what exactly?

ELOISE. That…we are just looking for girls that fall on the other end of the African skin spectrum.

HEADMISTRESS FRANCIS. Okay, wait a minute. Eloise… How can you—of all people—co-sign with that?!

ELOISE. Ummm… Big money! Big promotion! One step closer to owning the Miss Ghana pageant. Something a woman has never done!

HEADMISTRESS FRANCIS. Oh please, this isn't about women's equality, this is about you! And I'm not going to have my girls used as pawns for your nonsense.

ELOISE. *(A bit more tart.)* Hey, hey! This pageant is not nonsense. It is an amazing opportunity for a girl from our country to travel the world and represent Ghana. I feel insulted that you would doubt my efforts. The MGU platform is a highly respected one.

HEADMISTRESS FRANCIS. Platform?! Please!

ELOISE. Listen Francis—

HEADMISTRESS FRANCIS. —You haven't changed one bit since secondary school. If it doesn't benefit you, who cares!

ELOISE. That's right! And look at what that attitude has afforded me, darling! I'm Miss Ghana 1966. And here you are, still trying to keep up with the popular girls.

HEADMISTRESS FRANCIS. And here you are, still trying to be one.

Paulina walks into the cafeteria.

PAULINA. Oh, uh, good afternoon Headmistress.

HEADMISTRESS FRANCIS. Paulina, what are you doing out of class?

PAULINA. Sister Donkor was not feeling well, so she dismissed us a few minutes early... Hello!

ELOISE. *(Curt.)* Hello.

HEADMISTRESS FRANCIS. Ah yes Paulina. This is Eloise Amponsah: Miss Ghana 1966. She's this year's recruiter for the Miss Ghana pageant.

PAULINA. Wow! Miss Ghana 1966! In the flesh! I can't believe it.

ELOISE. Oh thank you dear. Paulina, you said?

PAULINA. Yes. Paulina Sarpong. I am in my last year here at Aburi...

ELOISE. How lovely.

PAULINA. We were not expecting you until tomorrow.

ELOISE. Oh, well I was just so anxious to see what Aburi had to offer, I couldn't wait.

PAULINA. *(Here's her chance—very rehearsed and polished.)* I see. Well, I believe that it has always been my calling to do something influential. If I was chosen to be Miss Ghana, God will use me as a vessel to show the world how beautiful our country is and change the stereotypes of how Africans are perceived.

ELOISE. Thank you…for that.

PAULINA. You're welcome.

HEADMISTRESS FRANCIS. Eh, Paulina, please tell Miss Amponsah more about your achievements here at school.

PAULINA. Ah yes, well, I am very involved: I'm on the debate team, the table tennis club, and I am the lead soloist in the show choir. I'm also in a long-term relationship with a Ghana Black Star soccer player.

ELOISE. Ooh, an athlete. Hold on to that one.

PAULINA. Oh, I plan to. I know Kofi is my true love.

HEADMISTRESS FRANCIS. Personally, I think Paulina would make for a great contestant in the pageant.

ELOISE. Sure. *(To Paulina.)* How tall are you, love?

PAULINA. Oh I can be any height you need me to be with right pair of high-heeled shoes.

ELOISE. *(Small dismissive laugh.)* And I can see you don't have a problem with your weight—

HEADMISTRESS FRANCIS. Miss Amponsah—

ELOISE. —These things are important to note Headmistress.

PAULINA. Well I work out nearly every day and always try to eat appropriately.

ELOISE. Oh, you are ahead of the game because trust me, it doesn't get any easier when you are my age.

PAULINA. Which cannot be a day over twenty-five. Surely you were too young to compete the first time around.

ELOISE. *(Slightly flattered.)* Awww… How cute.

HEADMISTRESS FRANCIS. I have to say Miss Amponsah, I think you might be looking at your next Miss Ghana right here. See how she knows all the right things to say.

A school bell chimes.

ELOISE. Ah…that old, school bell. Hmm… Anyway, I look forward to seeing what you and the rest of the girls have to offer when I'm back tomorrow.

PAULINA. Me too. And again, it really was such an honor meeting you.

ELOISE. Thank you love. Well, let me get going now.

HEADMISTRESS FRANCIS. Here, let me show you out, Miss Amponsah.

Headmistress and Eloise start to exit as Nana enters the cafeteria.

NANA. Good afternoon Headmistress.

HEADMISTRESS FRANCIS. Hello Nana.

NANA. I was just about to head to the front office. You still need me to sort all of those records by the end of the day, yes?

HEADMISTRESS FRANCIS. Uh…yes. But let me just see this guest out.

NANA. Yes Headmistress.

Headmistress and Eloise exit. Nana and Paulina are by themselves. Awkward beat.

PAULINA. So…were you able to—

Nana reaches into her book sack and pulls out a folder.

NANA. Here.

PAULINA. Great.

Nana stares at Paulina as she starts to look through the files. (Noticing Nana.) You can go now.

Nana begins to leave.

Oh and Nana?

NANA. Yes?

PAULINA. I've decided…you can't be a part of the group anymore. You're not really mixing with our…aesthetic. Come check in with me when you've dropped about fifteen to twenty pounds, okay? … Good luck.

Nana is about to leave again, but stops herself.

NANA. You know what Paulina…

PAULINA. *(Sighs—can't be bothered.)* What?

NANA. You're not as special as you think you are!

PAULINA. I'm not?

NANA. No! You're not. And I can't believe that I used to feel lucky that I was your friend! That I was actually proud that you claimed me. But you know what? I am lucky. Because I will never, ever be you!

Small beat.

PAULINA. *(Dismissive.)* Nana… Of course you won't.

Nana runs off as Ericka enters the cafeteria. Paulina is busy reading the file and doesn't immediately notice Ericka walk in.

ERICKA. Hey Paulina.

Paulina stuffs the folder in her bag.

PAULINA. Hi… What are you doing here?

ERICKA. Just waiting for the girls. They told me to meet them here so we could walk over to the dorm together.

PAULINA. Oh that's right. Your little "makeover party."

ERICKA. …Yeah… You can come too you know? Open invitation.

PAULINA. No, I'm okay. I have more important things to do.

ERICKA. Well, if you change your mind, you can always—

PAULINA. I won't.

ERICKA. …Okay.

Silence. Beat. Neither of them knows what to do. Ericka takes a bar of chocolate out of her bag.

Want some chocolate?

PAULINA. No… Calories.

ERICKA. Right.

PAULINA. Also, you should know that any sort of sweet is not allowed on campus or in the dormitories. It's considered contraband.

ERICKA. Oh…I thought we all just knew to keep it a secret.

PAULINA. Secrets, eh? Is that your thing?

ERICKA. No… But it's just chocolate.

PAULINA. Right. Your daddy's cocoa. Do you have an endless supply?

ERICKA. Not really.

Ericka shifts.

PAULINA. I've driven past that property. Nice mansion.

ERICKA. Didn't spend much time there.

PAULINA. Ah, yes. America. Ohio. Don't you think your friends miss you?

ERICKA. I don't know. I had a pretty small circle.

PAULINA. I know the feeling… It's not like we just let anyone into our group.

ERICKA. Oh… Is there a test you need to pass or something?

PAULINA. *(Amused.)* Listen…Ericka. You're new here, so let me help you understand some things: I have been running this school for a long time. Nothing and no one crosses me.

ERICKA. Okay.

PAULINA. And no one cares about your makeup, or music and fancy American things.

ERICKA. Clearly you do.

PAULINA. Excuse me?

ERICKA. You're the one who keeps bringing it up. Why do you care so much?

PAULINA. I don't.

ERICKA. You sure about that?

PAULINA. Very.

ERICKA. Listen Paulina—I don't know what your problem is, but I'm not afraid of you, okay? It's going to take a lot more than some empty threats to shake me.

PAULINA. No threats here. Just a warning.

ERICKA. Sure.

> *Ama, Mercy, and Gifty enter the cafeteria.*

MERCY and GIFTY. Hi/Hey Paulina.

AMA. Ericka! You ready to head over to the dorm?

MERCY and GIFTY. Makeover party!

> *Paulina sucks teeth loudly. She pushes past Ama, Mercy, and Gifty to exit.*

AMA. What's her problem now?

ERICKA. Not sure.

MERCY. Probably another one of her mood swings.

AMA. *(Rolls eyes.)* Always something with her.

GIFTY. Well let's go! I'm ready for this makeover party!

MERCY. Can't wait to see your dress options Ericka!

GIFTY. Honestly, we never really liked the ones that Paulina's aunt sent anyway.

ERICKA. Is that the one who works at White Castle?

Ama and Ericka laugh. Mercy and Gifty are confused.

MERCY and GIFTY. What?

AMA. Ericka told me about that place and you guys, it is FAR from being a castle.

MERCY. Whaaaat?

GIFTY. No?! For true?!

AMA. They sell fast food there.

ERICKA. Burgers and fries.

MERCY and GIFTY. Like McDonald's?

ERICKA. But not…

AMA. Oh… And Chinatown…

ERICKA. All they sell there are knockoffs.

MERCY and GIFTY. Knockoffs?

AMA. It's all fake! But Ericka has the real stuff.

ERICKA. Calvin Klein. From Macy's department store.

MERCY. Woooooow.   GIFTY. A store with departments.

ERICKA. That's right. And you girls are going to look amazing!

MERCY. Wow. Ericka, it's like you were sent from heaven.

GIFTY. A dress angel.

ERICKA. Oh, come on.

GIFTY. It's true. We are going to kill this audition.

MERCY. Yeah. And we have the list of sample questions that the recruiter might ask. I'm feeling very nervous about that section.

ERICKA. Oh, come on Mercy. It can't be that bad? Let's just practice one, yeah?

GIFTY. Yesss! Rehearsal! This is great. *(To Ericka.)* Okay, so you be the host and we'll be the audience. Here, sit Ama.

ERICKA. Okay… You ready?

MERCY. No…

GIFTY. You got this cousin!

ERICKA. *(Reads.)* "So, if you could be either fire or water, what would you be and why?"

MERCY. Well…I am a human being and I do not know how it is to be fire or water. And for that reason, I really do not have an answer to this because as you see, I am a human being. I am a girl who has emotions and fire and water do not. So…

> *All the girls laugh.*

ERICKA. So…we'll practice a bunch of times tonight.

MERCY. Good. I'm going to need it.

AMA. And those questions are silly anyway Mercy.

GIFTY. AND it doesn't matter how we answer the questions, because the recruiter will be too focused on our amazing dresses!

ERICKA. That's right. So let's head over to my dorm and pick some looks!

ALL GIRLS. Yes! Makeover party!

ERICKA. You girls want some chocolate?

ALL GIRLS. Oooh! Yeah!

> *They all laugh and head out excitedly.*

PART THREE

Paulina enters the cafeteria to her own fanfare. She's dressed in a lovely dress, pageant-ready.

PAULINA. "And now, please welcome, Miss Ghana 1986 contestant, Paulina Sarpong."

(To herself.) And applause, applause, applause. Okay, then remember to stand straight, smile and look like you're having an amazing time.

Plastic smile as she reads the sample card.

"What would you do to change the image of Ghana if you were selected to be in the Miss Global Universe Pageant?"

(To herself.) "Should I be crowned, it will be"... no, "I will make it my mission to become influential in our political government"... no, "our political community to make Ghana stand out as an African nation that has thrived since our freedom"... "Our independence"... Yeah, that's good. Look confident. Be confident. You got this Paulina. This is yours. This. Is. Yours.

Paulina looks around, pulls out a small container of lotion and rubs it on her face. It stings, but she continues to rub it in anyway. Nana sees Paulina putting on the cream, but makes sure she's out of Paulina's sight. After a moment, Nana enters. She is dressed in her Sunday's best as well. She looks at Paulina, and then moves to sit at a table away from her.

Nana.

NANA. Paulina.

Silence.

Ready for the pageant?

PAULINA. I've been ready.

NANA. Sure.

Silence.

PAULINA. Look at you... Your dress is actually...pretty nice.

NANA. I know.

Silence.

…You know… My hands are a little dry. Do you have any cream?

PAULINA. No.

NANA. You sure?

> *Ericka, Ama, Mercy, and Gifty enter the cafeteria, laughing and carrying on. They are all dressed in their Sunday's best as well. Ericka and Paulina look the best by far.*

ERICKA. Don't worry Mercy. Your hair looks great!

MERCY. Oh God, I'm so nervous.

GIFTY. *(Spotting Nana.)* Hey Nana!

AMA. You look so pretty!

ALL GIRLS. Yes!/Hey Nana!/Look at you!/Eh hehn!

NANA. Thanks girls.

PAULINA. *(Sarcasm.)* Heh… Pretty.

MERCY and GIFTY. This girl!/Heh—this one here.

AMA. Paulina.

PAULINA. Awww… Look at you girls. *(Amused.)* I'm sure you'll get points for effort.

AMA. And look at you Paulina?! That knockoff Calvin Klean looks great.

> *The girls snicker.*

PAULINA. Actually, this is a new designer. I like to keep up with the hottest fashions.

AMA. Oh really?

PAULINA. Yeah, you know I'm a trendsetter.

MERCY. Here she goes. Still telling lies!

GIFTY. Running her mouth again!

AMA. Well, we're glad today is the audition. Gives you a chance to take a break from spreading rumors about us all over school.

PAULINA. Me?! Whatever.

MERCY and GIFTY. Yeah, you!

MERCY. Spreading rumors!

GIFTY. And rumors hurt!

PAULINA. Please. I have better things to do.

AMA. Then why did you start telling everyone in our dormitory AGAIN that I'm not a virgin?! You KNOW that's not true!

PAULINA. I don't know what you do to keep Osei.

GIFTY. Or that I'm cheating in English class?

PAULINA. Everyone knows you can't read Gifty!

GIFTY. I'm getting better!

MERCY. Or telling everyone that I'm lying about my father being a doctor!

PAULINA. Why else would he let you dress like you're from the bush?!

AMA. Well at least she knows who her father is.

MERCY and GIFTY. Yeah!

PAULINA. Excuse me?

AMA. Tell me, has your mother figured it out yet? Or is she still busy spreading her legs for every man in your village?

PAULINA. Wow Ama?! After all I have done for you.

AMA. All you've done?! You talk about all of us like we're dogs! I'm supposed to be your best friend and look at what you say about me, my family, and my boyfriend!

PAULINA. He's trash Ama.

AMA. At least he is real!

PAULINA. What?

AMA. Everyone with half a brain can figure out that you have been making Kofi up!

PAULINA. No I haven't!

AMA. He never calls for you.

MERCY. Never!

AMA. Never shows up to the dances.

GIFTY. Never!

AMA. And I don't know how you get these letters he allegedly sends. I work in the mail room and I've never seen a letter come for you even once! They all just magically appear!

MERCY and GIFTY. Magic!

PAULINA. I have ALWAYS known you were jealous of me Ama!

AMA. Of what?!

PAULINA. Everything! You want to dress like me, act like me, be me!

AMA. You don't even want to be yourself!

PAULINA. Yeah, okay.

AMA. Tell me… How many times did Headmistress have to send you to hospital our first year, eh? Your face full of blisters and blood from all the bleaching cream you would use!

MERCY. What? GIFTY. Bleaching cream?!

PAULINA. Ama… You promised—

AMA. —No! I'm done covering for you! Everyone should know the truth Paulina! And the truth is you hate yourself so much, you would do ANYTHING to change!

PAULINA. Well, since we're being all honest!: Do the girls know that your father is in prison? That the pastor was stealing money from his own church?!

MERCY and GIFTY. Whaaaaat?

AMA. You are such a—

PAULINA. A what?!

ERICKA. Paulina, that's enough!

PAULINA. Oh, you don't want me to get started on you Ericka!

ERICKA. You need to relax, okay?!

PAULINA. And you need to stay out of my way! I will take you down you too!

ERICKA. Oh yeah?

PAULINA. Yeah! So don't fuck with me!, sweetie!

The girls hear Headmistress coming down the hall.

ALL GIRLS. Eh-Eh!/She's coming!/She's here!/I'm so nervous.

Headmistress Francis and Eloise enter the cafeteria. The girls play nice for them.

HEADMISTRESS FRANCIS. Oh my goodness! Look at how lovely you girls look!

ALL GIRLS. Thank you Headmistress.

HEADMISTRESS FRANCIS. Girls, I would like to introduce you to Ms. Eloise Amponsah—former Miss Ghana 1966. She is one of the recruiters for this year's pageant.

ELOISE. Good afternoon ladies. It is such a pleasure to meet you all.

ALL GIRLS. Thank you Ms. Amponsah.

PAULINA. Yes! It is very nice to see you again.

ELOISE. *(Dismissive.)* Yes.

HEADMISTRESS FRANCIS. Right, you remember Paulina. And this here is Ama.

AMA. Hello.

HEADMISTRESS FRANCIS. Mercy and Gifty.

MERCY.	GIFTY.
Good afternoon.	We are happy to receive you.

HEADMISTRESS FRANCIS. Our shy little Nana here.

NANA. Hello ma'am.

ELOISE. Ma'am? Oh please, save that for my mother. And Headmistress, who is this lovely young lady? What is your name?

ERICKA. Ericka Boafo.

HEADMISTRESS FRANCIS. She just recently transferred into the school from The States.

ELOISE. America?! Wow.

ERICKA. Yes, but I have returned to Ghana now to complete my studies here, in my home country.

Paulina laughs.

HEADMISTRESS FRANCIS. Paulina.

PAULINA. Sorry. She just made me think of…sorry, it's nothing. My apologies.

HEADMISTRESS FRANCIS. Now, as I told you Eloise, the girls picked this song themselves and have been working on it all week in preparation for this audition.

ELOISE. Lovely.

HEADMISTRESS FRANCIS. Now Ericka here hasn't had time to

rehearse with us but she says she knows the song very well. *(To Ericka.)* So just do the best you can, okay?

ERICKA. I will.

HEADMISTRESS FRANCIS. Great! Ms. Amponsah, please have a seat here.

ELOISE. Thank you.

HEADMISTRESS FRANCIS. Okay now, let's get into formation here and when I point to you, step out to sing your part. Ama— why don't we start with you.

> *The girls all stand in formation with Ama up center.*

Now, straight backs, chests up, and just let the music float out of you. Here we go.

> *Headmistress Francis blows the note into her pitch pipe and cues the girls. They all sing a unison "Oooo" a cappella. (It's "The Greatest Love of All.")**

AMA. *(Earnest.)*
> *I believe de children are de future.*
> *Teach dem well and let dem lead the way.*
> *Show dem all de beauty they posses inside.*

HEADMASTER FRANCIS. Nana.

NANA. *(Barely audible.)*
> *Give dem a sense of pride to make it easier,*
> *Let de children's laughter remind us how we used to be.*

HEADMISTRESS FRANCIS. Gifty.

> *Gifty steps up, smiling with confidence.*

GIFTY. *(Not good but very confident.)*
> *Everybody's searching for a hero,*
> *People need someone to look up to.*
> *I never found anyone who fulfilled that need.*

HEADMISTRESS FRANCIS. Get ready Mercy. You are next.

GIFTY.
> *A lonely place to be.*
> *So I learned to depend on me.*

---

* See Special Note on Songs/Recordings on page 62.

MERCY. *(Too high-pitched.)*
> *I decided long ago*
> *Never to walk in anyone's shadow.*

HEADMISTRESS FRANCIS. Eh-eh Mercy! Just bring your key down.

MERCY. *(Too low.)*
> *If I fail, if I succeed,*
> *At least I'll live as I believe.*
> *No matter what they take from me,*
> *They can't take away my dignity.*

HEADMISTRESS FRANCIS. *(Another blow into the pitch pipe.)* Okay, everyone.

ALL GIRLS.
> *Because the greatest love of all is happening to me.*
> *I found the greatest love of all inside of me.*

HEADMISTRESS FRANCIS. Okay, Paulina's next…

> Paulina steps to the front, full of all the confidence she can muster.

PAULINA. *(It's lovely.)*
> *I believe the children are our future.*
> *Teach them well and let them lead the way.*
> *Show them all the beauty they possess inside.*

HEADMISTRESS FRANCIS. Ericka you're next dear.

PAULINA. *(More confident.)*
> *Give them a sense of pride to make it easier.*
> *Let the children's laughter remind us how we used to be.*

> Ericka steps in front of Paulina.

ERICKA. *(Channeling Whitney—her voice is amazing.)*
> *I decided long ago,*
> *Never to walk in anyone's shadow.*
> *If I fail,*
> *If I succeed*
> *At least I'll live as I believe.*
> *No matter what they take from me.*
> *They can't take away my dignity.*

ELOISE. *(Inspired!)* Praise God!

ALL GIRLS.

Because the greatest love of all	*Ericka is ad libbing*
Is happening to me.	*and riffing to her*
I found the greatest love of all	*heart's content.*
Inside of me.	

> *All of the girls, except Paulina, start to clap, cheer, and praise Ericka. Paulina begins to hyperventilate—she's about to explode.*

ELOISE. Bravo! Ericka! You are quite a talent! You would make quite the splash at the Miss Ghana pageant!

> *The girls all cheer for Ericka again, then—*

PAULINA. NOOOOOOO!!!

HEADMISTRESS FRANCIS. Eh-eh! Paulina. Calm yourself!

PAULINA. NO! SHE CAN'T BE THE NEXT MISS GHANA BECAUSE SHE IS NOT EVEN A REAL GHANAIAN!

MERCY. You say what?   GIFTY. Eh-eh! how?

PAULINA. She was born in America! Her mother is white! Ericka Johnson!

ERICKA. What?!

PAULINA. Boafo isn't even her real name!

MERCY and GIFTY. Wooooooow!

HEADMISTRESS FRANCIS. Paulina!

PAULINA. It's in her file!

HEADMISTRESS FRANCIS. Her file?!

PAULINA. She's a bastard! Her father only claimed her now because her mother is dead!

HEADMISTRESS FRANCIS. I can't believe this!

ERICKA. Who the hell do you think you are?!

PAULINA. I said to not mess with me, didn't I?!

HEADMISTRESS FRANCIS. Hey! Girls, stop this!

AMA. This is a new low / even for you! Paulina!

ERICKA. —That is none of your business!

PAULINA. No one wants you here! Not even your own father!

HEADMISTRESS FRANCIS. Paulina, enough!

PAULINA. Why are you yelling at me? Nana gave me her file!

HEADMISTRESS FRANCIS. What?!

AMA. Nana!

HEADMISTRESS FRANCIS. Is that true?

NANA. I can explain Headmistress.

PAULINA. And that's not the first time!

NANA. No, I only did it for you!

PAULINA. Was that before or after you erased all of your detention marks?

HEADMISTRESS FRANCIS. Excuse me?!

NANA. That is not true / Headmistress!

PAULINA. —It is true! She said you were trying to keep her from getting into college!

HEADMISTRESS FRANCIS. Unbelievable! This is unbelievable!

Something is going on with Paulina's face.

ELOISE. Franny, I don't know what's going on, but can I just pick someone and skedaddle—

PAULINA. Well it can't be Ericka! The rules clearly state that you have to be BORN IN GHANA to REAL GHANAIAN parents! No knockoffs!

ELOISE. Knockoffs?!

Paulina is now fully concerned with what is going on with her face. It's burning or bleeding or something. She continues to try to cover it.

ERICKA. You are so disgusting Paulina! Everything everyone says / about you is true!

AMA. —You are so crazy and desperate / Paulina!

MERCY. This is why we didn't borrow your dresses!

GIFTY. You are crazy and desperate!

ELOISE. Ericka… Is this true?

ERICKA. Well…

41

AMA. It's probably another lie! That's all Paulina does!

MERCY and GIFTY. Spread rumors and lies!

> *Beat.*

HEADMISTRESS FRANCIS. Paulina…

> *Paulina's face is now blistering and bleeding.*

MERCY. Eh-eh, is that blood?

GIFTY. Blood?!

ELOISE. —Yes, what is going on there?

HEADMISTRESS FRANCIS. Ama get me a bowl of cold water and a washcloth. Now!

NANA. —You wish you looked like Ericka!

PAULINA. Shut up Nana!

NANA. NO! You shut up Paulina!

> *Nana walks up to Paulina and snatches the cream from her dress.*

PAULINA. Give me that!

MERCY and GIFTY. Eh-eh! Bleaching cream!

NANA. I AM SO SICK OF YOUR SHIT!

HEADMISTRESS FRANCIS. Hey. Hey! Stop it!

MERCY. Nana!

GIFTY. She said "shit"!

ERICKA. CAN'T YOU SEE PAULINA?! You're a fucking bitch! That's why everyone hates you!

HEADMISTRESS FRANCIS. Ericka!

PAULINA. And you are a half-caste bastard!

HEADMISTRESS FRANCIS. HEY! THAT IS ENOUGH!… I CANNOT BELIEVE THIS! This is absolutely REPREHENSIBLE behavior! You should all be ashamed of yourselves!

ALL GIRLS. *(Eventually.)* Sorry Headmistress.

HEADMISTRESS FRANCIS. Eloise, I assure you this is far and beyond their usual characters.

ELOISE. I would hope so.

HEADMISTRESS FRANCIS. Can you please step out for a moment? I need to deal with all of this.

ELOISE. …Sure.

Eloise shakes her head, mainly at Ericka, and walks off.

HEADMISTRESS FRANCIS. Paulina and Ericka, you two sit down. And the rest of you—report straight to your dormitories. And be prepared because ALL of you will be receiving several detentions for your actions today!

ALL GIRLS. Yes Headmistress.

The girls start to exit. Nana walks over to Headmistress and hands her the container of bleaching cream.

NANA. Should I give this to you?

HEADMISTRESS FRANCIS. Uh, yes, I'll take it Nana. Now go.

Nana exits. All of the girls are gone. Headmistress stares at the container and then puts it on the table between Paulina and Ericka.

I mean, I don't even know where to begin with this. Of all the years I have been Headmistress of this school, I have never seen anything like this. Stealing files! Foul language! Fighting! All of which are grounds for expulsion!

ERICKA.	PAULINA.
I didn't do—	Headmistress, she was—

HEADMISTRESS FRANCIS. Eh-eh! I did not ask either of you to speak!

Have I not gone above and beyond for you girls? Eh?

Paulina—I have looked after you like you are my own child. Took care of you and paid for things your mother couldn't afford. And let's not talk about the countless hospital bills I incurred only for you to turn around and start using this mess again?

And you Ericka. I know this has been a very tough time for you, but fighting is not the way to deal with these feelings—

ERICKA.	PAULINA.
Headmistress—	Look, she was the one—

HEADMISTRESS FRANCIS. I am not finished!

Now…while you two are students at my school, your studies will be your number-one and ONLY priority! Understand?

> *Ericka and Paulina nod.*

Now, I'm going to go find Eloise and when I come back, you two better have fixed this or no one is going to the pageant. Do I make myself clear?

ERICKA. Yes Headmistress.   PAULINA. Yes Headmistress.

HEADMISTRESS FRANCIS. Good.

> *Headmistress Francis exits. Paulina and Ericka sit in silence for a long beat.*
>
> *Paulina bursts into tears. Ericka turns away and perhaps some tears are shed too.*

ERICKA. You crossed the line!

PAULINA. Well, I'm not sorry! Ms. Amponsah should know the truth. It is against the rules.

ERICKA. Please! This isn't about the pageant!

PAULINA. It's the truth!

ERICKA. If you don't like me, fine! But you had no right to—

PAULINA. —You stole all of my friends!

ERICKA. That's how you treat your friends?

PAULINA. You came in here, acting like you've got everything—

ERICKA. —Lotion and makeup?!—

PAULINA. —Like you didn't have a care in the world!

ERICKA. Listen you don't know SHIT about my life okay?!—

PAULINA. —Oh really?—

ERICKA. —NOTHING! I wasn't rich. I didn't have friends.

PAULINA. Whatever.

ERICKA. You think those white kids wanted anything to do with me? You think there were any other black kids in Portsmouth?! I was always alone! …And my father…was here. With his cocoa factory… And his wife and children. Living this perfect life… Not even thinking about me… Ashamed of me… His white daughter.

PAULINA. Oh please.

ERICKA. And you think my life was easy? My mother is all I had—
…And you try watching your mother die and talk to me about how easy that is…

Did you ever stop to think that I might be jealous of you?!

Paulina sucks teeth loudly.

That you know where you come from? …That you have a family?

I'm sorry that you don't see how lucky you are.

PAULINA. Lucky? Are you serious? Lucky where?! That my mother has eight children, most of us with different fathers? Lucky that we are the poorest people in our village? Lucky to be the darkest one in my family? That even with our little bit of money, my mother gave me bleaching cream instead of food—'cause that would "serve me better in life"?!… That's not luck Ericka, okay?! The only luck I had was getting a scholarship to Aburi.

Small beat.

And you… You're the daughter of one of the richest men in the country. You will always have something… Always…

Small beat.

…Trust me—my mother would have gladly traded me in for you… Clearly…
She was right.

ERICKA. No she wasn't.

PAULINA. No, she was… Listen, the world has already decided… You are better than me.

ERICKA. That's not true.

PAULINA. Ericka… Yes it is.

> *They sit in silence. After a moment, Headmistress Francis and Eloise enter the cafeteria.*

HEADMISTRESS FRANCIS. I'm back girls. And I believe you have something to say to Ms. Amponsah?

PAULINA. Yes. We are very sorry for our behavior Ms. Amponsah.

ERICKA. Yes, very sorry. This will never happen again.

ELOISE. Thank you. But trust me, I understand how heated things can get when it comes to competition. After all, I am Miss Ghana

1966 and I did not get that prestigious title without getting a bit of dirt on my hands.

HEADMISTRESS FRANCIS. Now, I've already asked Ms. Amponsah if she would like to come back another day to make a decision, but—

ELOISE. Oh no, no, no. This is time-sensitive.

HEADMISTRESS FRANCIS. Right.

ELOISE. Now, besides that "episode," you have a lovely group of girls, but it's clear the standouts are certainly Paulina and Ericka here. Though in light of what Paulina has discovered, Ericka would be disqualified if the MGU committee found out.

HEADMISTRESS FRANCIS. Yes, I understand.

ELOISE. …And that is why we are not going to tell them.

PAULINA. What?

ERICKA. …What?

HEADMISTRESS FRANCIS. Eloise, now wait just a minute here. You can't do that.

ELOISE. Oh, I can…and I will.

HEADMISTRESS FRANCIS. Well I won't allow it! I will call the MGU committee myself if I have to.

ELOISE. Listen, I don't have time for this! I've got a pageant I need to win.

HEADMISTRESS FRANCIS. But… Like this?

ELOISE. Well, you can't get anywhere in this world by playing fair.

HEADMISTRESS FRANCIS. So you would ruin these girls' dreams because of something this stupid?!

ELOISE. Yes, because I want to win!

HEADMISTRESS FRANCIS. But you won! Eloise, they named YOU Miss Ghana!

ELOISE. Yes, and once I left Ghana, no one cared! Those MGU judges didn't even blink my way! I might as well have been invisible! So if I have to push every darkie out of the way, so be it! I want my damn promotion! I want, for once in my life, to FINALLY be seen!

> *Beat.*

(Composes herself.) And anyway, I'm not the only person who will benefit here. If Ericka wins Miss Ghana, she gets the crown, Aburi gets a generous donation, and Ghana will FINALLY get some real recognition on a global platform. How is that not a win-win for everyone?!

HEADMISTRESS FRANCIS. It's not for Paulina—

ELOISE. Oh who cares about— *(Remembers—then sweetly.)* Listen, Paulina…dear. You are a beautiful and bright young lady. And I think you would make a fine candidate for the Miss Ghana pageant… Next year.

PAULINA. *(Trying to control her tears.)* Okay.

ELOISE. I can't make any promises on whether you'll be selected, but I am Miss Ghana 1966 and my recommendation will hold some weight.

PAULINA. Okay.

ELOISE. But…I can't speak for what I will do if you don't keep that mouth of yours shut about all of this… Do you understand?

PAULINA. *(Eventually.)* Yes.

ELOISE. Good… Do we all have an understanding?

ERICKA. Yeah.

HEADMISTRESS FRANCIS. *(Eventually.)* Yes.

ELOISE. *(Re: Ericka.)* Good. Now…I can't wait to show the recruiting team the diamond that I found in this mine! *(To Paulina.)* Just you wait Paulina. You will see all of the doors that Ericka is going to open for you! She is going to put Ghana on the map! You'll be thanking her—trust me! *(Back to Ericka.)* Now dear, let's talk about dresses…

> *Ericka and Eloise walk off. After a moment, Headmistress Francis sits down next to Paulina. Paulina begins to sob as Headmistress Francis pulls her into an embrace.*

EPILOGUE

Mercy and Gifty sit at the cafeteria table.

MERCY. Really good. Now let's—

GIFTY. Can we hurry up? It's almost time for the pageant!

MERCY. I know, but let's just read these next sentences and then we'll be done.

GIFTY. *(Sighs.)* Okay. *(Reads.)* "Are you there God, it's me Margaret. I'm in my new debroom—"

MERCY. Bedroom.

GIFTY. "Bedroom… But I still have the same deb."

MERCY. Bed.

GIFTY. "Bed… It's so quiet here at…night."

MERCY. Really, really good Gifty.

GIFTY. Thank you.

MERCY. You see? You just had to take your time with it.

GIFTY. Yeah, and this Judy Blume knows her stuff.

MERCY. You know, now that Headmistress is having that library built on campus, we should ask her for more books like this.

GIFTY. Yeah… Books. Anyway, where is everyone? This is the MISS GLOBAL UNIVERSE PAGEANT!

MERCY. I know.

GIFTY. And Headmistress promised that we could watch it after last period!

MERCY. I'm sure Headmistress is on her way Gifty.

GIFTY. This anxiety is too much, oh!

Nana walks into the cafeteria. She sits at the table.

MERCY and GIFTY. Nana!/Hey!/We haven't seen you in forever!

NANA. Hey girls.

MERCY. Finally off detentions.

NANA. I know. Finally done.

GIFTY. We thought we'd never see you again!

MERCY. I can't imagine. Being on detentions for two whole months—

GIFTY. —Sixty days—

MERCY. —No food.

NANA. —I had food.

GIFTY. —No water.

NANA. —It wasn't a dungeon you guys.

MERCY. —It basically was!

GIFTY. —Basically.

MERCY. —Going from class then straight to the office to work.

GIFTY. —Eating lunch—

MERCY. —With Headmistress just watching over you like—

> *Both Mercy and Gifty imitate what they think the stare was like.*

NANA. You guys are so silly.

MERCY. Glad that Headmistress saw that we weren't involved in all of that.

GIFTY. I don't know if my spirit could take two months of detentions.

NANA. I'm just glad it's over.

MERCY. Yeah… Anyway, it feels like we have so much to catch up on. What's going on with you?

NANA. Well—

MERCY. Ooh! So I was able to convince my dad to let me and Gifty stay here.

GIFTY. *(Touched.)* Uncle James is the best.

MERCY. After "Audition Day" things were touch and go.

GIFTY. Touch and go.

MERCY. But I had to explain to him, just sit him down and talk straight business, you know? Daughter to father. *(Maybe emotional… but like fake emotions.)* And it was hard, oh. Trying to explain to him how it is to be the child of a doctor, at one of the best schools in Ghana, trying to get good grades, look after my cousin…

…and not have new shoes…

GIFTY. …So hard…

MERCY. But I promised him that Gifty and I would stay out of trouble and get good grades for the rest of year. AND! He said if we do that, he MIGHT get me and Gifty…you're not going to believe this Nana…

NANA. What?

MERCY. A new pair of Nikes!!!!!!!

Mercy and Gifty celebrate.

GIFTY. Can you believe it?!

MERCY. I can already feel how good they will be on my feet.

GIFTY. So good.

NANA. That's amazing. Congrats.

MERCY. Oh! And Gifty is reading now! And she's pretty good too. She just finished her first book.

NANA. Really?!

GIFTY. Yes! *The Baby-Sitters Club.* Really powerful stuff.

NANA. Good for you.

MERCY. Anyway, enough about us, what's been up with you Nana?

NANA. *(Kind of proud.)* Well, Headmistress is letting me join the soccer team next week. I'm going to be playing goalie. I'm really excited about it.

MERCY. That's nice.

GIFTY. Good for you Nana.

NANA. Thanks. Headmistress thinks some extracurriculars will help with my college applications.

GIFTY. Speaking of—where is Headmistress?! The pageant!

MERCY. I'm sure she's coming Gifty, relax.

Ama walks into the cafeteria and comes to sit with the girls. Perhaps Gifty gets excited that it's the Headmistress, but is deflated when she sees Ama.

AMA. Nana. Finally free, eh?! Welcome back.

NANA. Thanks. It's good to be out again.

AMA. I'm sure.

NANA. I heard you got a few detentions too.

AMA. I did. Only for a week though. Which was fine. Working in the mail room is the worst. If I never have to see another envelope again for the rest of my life, I'll be okay.

> *The girls giggle.*

MERCY. Ama! Aren't you going to tell Nana the good news?

GIFTY. Hello!

AMA. Oh yeah, I got accepted to University of Ghana—early decision!

NANA. Wow Ama! That's amazing. Congratulations!

AMA. Thanks. I am still waiting to hear from the schools I applied to in America, but I'm really excited about U of G.

MERCY. Umm Ama, that is not the news we were talking about!

GIFTY. Yeah. Who cares about college?

AMA. What?

MERCY. *(Holds up left hand.)* GIFTY. *(Holds up left hand.)*
Uhh…hello!   Uhh…hello!

AMA. Oh, I mean, it's not even a big deal.

MERCY.   GIFTY.
Excuse me, yes it is!   Eh-eh! It's very big, oh!

AMA. But Osei told me that he wanted to make things official and…he proposed!

MERCY. Ahhhh!   GIFTY. Ahhhh!

AMA. *(Calming them down.)* It was supposed to be a secret you guys! We said we'd wait to share the news with our friends until after we told our parents. So we're not official yet.

MERCY. You might as well be!

GIFTY. And you better claim him.

MERCY. Because if you don't—

GIFTY. We will!

> *The girls all laugh.*
> *They settle. Gifty looks out of the cafeteria.*
> *Small beat.*

NANA. So…has anyone seen Paulina?

AMA. Not really. Just in class.

MERCY. I heard that she is still really sad.

GIFTY. Very depressed.

NANA. I've barely seen her. Especially since she had to move dormitories.

MERCY. And to the scary dormitory too.

GIFTY. I heard Headmistress only puts delinquents in there.

MERCY. I heard she's barely eaten anything.

GIFTY. And it takes her a long time to get out of bed.

AMA. It's probably best that she's not around people. Maybe she's learned something.

NANA. You know, she wrote me a letter. Slipped it under my door.

MERCY. She wrote you one too?

GIFTY. Us too.

AMA. I'm sure Headmistress forced her to.

NANA. I can't believe she lied about all of that.

MERCY. Who would make up a story like that?

GIFTY. And so detailed.

MERCY. Right. That Ericka is not Ghanaian? White mother?

GIFTY. That is too much.

NANA. Did you write her back?

MERCY. Eh, I thought about it.

GIFTY. Thought.

MERCY. But I didn't.

GIFTY. Yeah, no.

MERCY. Still…I've decided to forgive her.

GIFTY. Clearly, she lost her mind.

NANA. You think she'll come out and watch today?

GIFTY. Well she didn't watch the Miss Ghana pageant.

MERCY. Who can blame her?

GIFTY. True.

AMA. You think Ericka will actually win the Miss Global Universe pageant?

NANA. You never know. I still think she's the best Miss Ghana we have ever had.

MERCY. Yeah she will AT LEAST make the top ten.

GIFTY. Top ten for sure.

> *Paulina, dressed in her school uniform but cloaked in a black shawl and sunglasses, enters the cafeteria.*

MERCY. Paulina! How are you?

GIFTY. Yeah. How's your heart?

MERCY. Are you okay?

GIFTY. Do you need something?

PAULINA. Ladies please. I am fine. It's just nice to be out in the fresh air again.

MERCY and GIFTY. Yeah/Of course/Sure, fresh air.

PAULINA. This has been a really difficult time on my spirit, you know? And I have done a lot of self-reflection ever since The Pageant. And I know God is working on me. With His grace, I will get through this.

MERCY and GIFTY. Amen.

PAULINA. *(Notices Nana and Ama.)* Nana…Ama.

NANA and AMA. Mmmm.

PAULINA. You…uh…got my letter, yes?

AMA. I did.   NANA. Yeah.

PAULINA. And…I know that we may never be friends again—

AMA. Nope.   NANA. Probably not.

PAULINA. Which is fine… Just know…that I'm sorry, okay?

AMA. Whatever.

NANA. Yeah okay.

> *Beat. They aren't quite sure what to do.*

MERCY. Well, we're glad to see you Paulina. We didn't know if you were going to come and watch.

GIFTY. Maybe you'd be too upset.

PAULINA. No, it's fine. Ericka won Miss Ghana. Good for her.

Headmistress Francis enters the cafeteria, wheeling on a TV cart. She turns it on, adjusts the television.

HEADMISTRESS FRANCIS. Girls! Can I get a bit of help here.

ALL GIRLS. *(Cheering, maybe except Paulina.)* Headmistress!/It's time! It's time!/We can't wait!

HEADMISTRESS FRANCIS. Well, good afternoon girls. Yes, I know you are all very excited.

ALL GIRLS. *(Maybe except Paulina.)* YES!

MERCY. *(Setting up the TV.)* Gifty! Get the cord. Eh-eh—don't tangle it.

GIFTY. I'm not! Just plug it in, oh.

Mercy and Gifty continue to fuss about the plug, the TV, the pageant, etc.

AMA. Nana, help me move this.

NANA. Okay. Ah, this is so exciting.

AMA. I know! Oh, don't forget the popcorn.

NANA. Got it!

HEADMISTRESS FRANCIS. What a day, eh? To see one of our very own Aburi School girls—on international television.

Gifty cannot contain her excitement.

MERCY. Oh my goodness! What if she wins?!

AMA. That would be amazing!

GIFTY. I know!

Gifty is losing it! All the girls, except Paulina, applaud. Paulina smiles.

HEADMISTRESS FRANCIS. Okay, are we all set up now?

ALL GIRLS. *(Over-excited!)* Yes!

Headmistress Francis turns on the television and turns up the volume. The girls all watch intently.

GHANAIAN TV ANNOUNCER. And now, Ghana News Network takes you back to the Miss Global Universe pageant broadcasting live from Orlando, Florida.

The girls all cheer. Maybe not Paulina.

AMERICAN TV HOST. Good evening ladies and gentlemen and welcome back to the Miss Global Universe pageant! We have people tuning in from all over the world tonight, isn't that exciting?

ALL GIRLS. Yes!

AMERICAN TV HOST. But not as exciting as announcing our top-ten semifinalists!

ALL GIRLS. Ahhh!!!

MERCY. They're already at the top ten!

GIFTY. I'm going to pass out!

MERCY. Do you see Ericka?

GIFTY. There's so many girls.

AMA. Shhh!

AMERICAN TV HOST. Our celebrity panel judged each young lady for poise and grace while they wore an evening gown of their own choice.

AMA. I wonder which designer Ericka wore?

MERCY. You think she knows Calvin Klein?!

GIFTY. Oh for sure!

AMA. Shhh!

AMERICAN TV HOST. Each judge personally interviewed each of our contestants with the aid of an interpreter when needed.

AMA. Interpreter?

NANA. Like they found someone who speaks Twi?

MERCY and GIFTY. Yeah right.

AMERICAN TV HOST. Now all of these scores will determine who will be our ten semifinalists. As you can see, I've been joined here onstage by all of our contestants.

MERCY. How many Africans do you see?

GIFTY. Eh-Eh! There's too many girls! And you know I can't count that fast!

AMA. Shhhh!

GIFTY. *(To Ama.)* You need to relax!

AMERICAN TV HOST. Now let me remind you folks at home that

these names will be read in no particular order and the competition scores will ONLY be shown to you at home.

ALL GIRLS. Exclusives!/Ehhh!/Us! Only us!

AMERICAN TV HOST. Here now are the names of our ten semi-finalists, all competing for the title of Miss Global Universe, 1986.

ALL GIRLS. *(Maybe except Paulina.)* Yaaay! / Ahhh! / My blood pressure, oh!

AMERICAN TV HOST. The first name on the list is…Miss Brazil.

> *Applause and cheesy '80s music (this happens after each contestant is announced).*

AMA. They gave her an 8.4!

NANA. What's the highest you can get?

AMA. Probably a 10.

AMERICAN TV HOST. I think the audience will like…Miss France.

MERCY. Which audience?

GIFTY. 'Cause I don't like her!

AMERICAN TV HOST. And let's welcome…Miss Italy.

NANA. Wow, she's got the lowest score so far, 8.2.

AMA. What are they even basing these scores on anyway?

MERCY and GIFTY. Who knows.

AMERICAN TV HOST. And now, come on down…

GIFTY. MISS GHANA!

AMERICAN TV HOST. Miss United States.

ALL GIRLS. Of course!

MERCY. 9.0! Please!

GIFTY. Yeah, please!

AMERICAN TV HOST. We're halfway there now with…Miss South Africa.

ALL GIRLS. Yaaay!/Wooo!/Finally! Someone from Africa!

NANA. Oh wait…you guys, she's a white.

ALL GIRLS. Again?!/These people!/Of course she is!

AMERICAN TV HOST. And here comes Miss Switzerland.

MERCY. 8.3?! With that crazy hair?!

GIFTY. Two words: Hot. Comb!

HEADMISTRESS FRANCIS. Gifty.

GIFTY. *(Under breath.)* It's true.

AMERICAN TV HOST. Next is Miss Venezuela!

ALL GIRLS. She's pretty./Not bad./Her hair is better than that other one at least./That dress! Wow!

AMERICAN TV HOST. Number eight on the list of semifinalists is…Miss Greece!

NANA. Hey! There's Ericka!

ALL GIRLS. *(Except Paulina.)* Ahhh!/Ericka is on television!/I can't believe it!/Oh my God!/She looks amazing!

HEADMISTRESS FRANCIS. Girls, please. You're going to miss the last two countries.

MERCY. One of them better be Ghana!

GIFTY. Because Miss Greece looks crazy!

AMERICAN TV HOST. Now ladies and gentlemen, we have two names to go and one of those names is…Miss Colombia.

NANA. Colombia?!

GIFTY. Where is that?

AMA. South America. You need to pay attention in geography Gifty.

GIFTY. SHHH!

AMERICAN TV HOST. And now number ten, the last contestant who has a chance to become Miss Global Universe…

ALL GIRLS. *(Except Paulina—scattered whispers.)* Ghana/Say Ghana/ If it's not Ghana, I will scream.

AMERICAN TV HOST. She is…Miss Sweden!

> *Everyone is stunned silent.*

Up next—the evening gown competition, featuring a performance by R&B star Bobby Brown!

> *Light applause and music is heard on the television. Headmistress lowers the volume on the television.*
>
> *Silence.*

HEADMISTRESS FRANCIS. Wow.

PAULINA. Wow.

MERCY. I can't believe it.

PAULINA. Yeah.

GIFTY. Maybe it's a mistake.

NANA. Ericka looked pretty though.

AMA. Not pretty enough.

> *Silence.*

HEADMISTRESS FRANCIS. Girls, I know you are disappointed… I am too. But look at the bright side—you got to see one of your own classmates on television, representing our country. That is a very big deal. And who knows, maybe next year things will be different.

PAULINA. Yeah…

AMA. Maybe.

GIFTY. I guess.

MERCY. So…all of that? For what?

NANA. All for nothing?

PAULINA. All for nothing.

> *Paulina turns up the volume on the television.*

AMERICAN TV HOST. And we're back folks with the top-ten most beautiful women in the world!

> *Thunderous applause from the television. It becomes louder and louder and louder…as the girls watch in silence. Lights fade.*

End of Play

PROPERTY LIST
(Use this space to create props lists for your production)

SOUND EFFECTS
(Use this space to create sound effects lists for your production)

Note on Songs/Recordings, Images, Other Production Design Elements

Performance rights to "The Greatest Love of All," written by Linda Creed and Michael Masser and originally performed by Whitney Houston, are included with the license to perform the play. Additional royalty fees for the use of the song will be automatically added to the license invoice. The use of the song and payment of the additional royalty fees is obligatory; no other song may be substituted. No changes may be made to the arrangement of the song, nor any changes to the lyrics, music, or other element of the song.

The following credits must appear in all playbills or programs in connection with presentation of the play:

"The Greatest Love of All"
Linda Creed, Michael Masser
Used by Permission of EMI Gold Horizon Music Corporation;
EMI Golden Torch Music Corporation
All Rights Reserved

Be advised that Dramatists Play Service neither holds the rights to nor grants permission to use any songs, recordings, images, or other design elements mentioned in the play other than "The Greatest Love of All." It is the responsibility of the producing theater/organization to obtain permission of the copyright owner(s) for any such use.

For any songs/recordings, images, or other design elements mentioned in the play other than "The Greatest Love of All," works in the public domain may be substituted. It is the producing theater/organization's responsibility to ensure the substituted work is indeed in the public domain. Dramatists Play Service cannot advise as to whether or not a song/arrangement/recording, image, or other design element is in the public domain.

NOTES
(Use this space to make notes for your production)

NOTES
(Use this space to make notes for your production)

NOTES
(Use this space to make notes for your production)